I have been writing
and illustrating this book
on the subject of grief
and survival almost daily
throughout this full year.
With love
and understanding of our journey,
my hope is that this book brings
comfort
to all who read it.

~ Claudia Chappel

First published by South Son Publishing, LLC™
Commerce Center-East Building
1777 Reisterstown Road, Suite 355
Baltimore, Maryland 21208

ISBN 978-1-7339047-2-8 Hardcover
ISBN 978-1-7339047-3-5 Paperback

In this book the author is simply giving a voice to the lessons she learned as she has come to terms with the loss of her son. She is not a trained psychiatrist, doctor, psychologist, grief counselor, or health care professional. She is not giving medical or psychological advice or counseling.

Please visit www.claudiachappel.com

Production assistance by Adam Robinson of Good Book Developers

An Illustrated Journey Through Grief

Claudia Chappel

S South Son Publishing™
Baltimore

Living life vibrantly
is possible
after the loss of a loved one,
in my case my son,
but do not let anyone rush you!
It takes a very long time
to build the strength needed
to even get off the couch
but in time you can
choose life.

As another day begins,
we have to continue navigating through our journey
trudging towards the light.
Why?
Because we have no other choice
I believe that my son is now resting in the light and
will be there when it's my time to join him.
Until then I will continue to try to lift
myself up and anyone else
who needs me.

This painting reminds me
of how it feels when you first lose your
child or mother or husband…
Trying to walk on uneven ground.
Your entire existence begins to turn upside down.
Even though life will never be the same,
the ground does level out
eventually.

I'll never forget
how I felt in the first few weeks
and months
after it happened.
Isolated, alone and
desperately sad.
When I did get out of the house
life felt so unreal.
I couldn't even imagine life
without him.
Eventually, I was able to return
to what I call,
my new normal.

When you are feeling alone
in your grief,
look around.
You are a beautiful flower in a field,
full of flowers
and next to you and all around
are thousands of others
feeling the same love and pain
as you.
The depth of your pain
mirrors the depth of your
loss and your
love.

I was a single mom.
I considered myself a mother lioness
protecting her young
and still my son died
before me.
I felt like I totally failed
as a mother.
I knew it wasn't my fault
but isn't the job of a mother to
protect her young?
These thoughts are dangerous
and destructive!
Just call them bad thoughts and
let them go!
They are deadly!!

So much in life is about choices.
No, I did not choose to have my son die before me.
At first all I wanted to do was die also.
That was not an acceptable choice
since it would destroy my daughter, his sister.
I had to set an example for her as to how to live
with our unthinkable tragedy,
our immense loss.
I chose the path of living well and as full as possible.
All paths end at the same place.
I choose the path that allows me to be
happy in spite of my grief.
Life is short,
the person you grieve for loved you too and would want
you to live vibrantly until he or she finds you again.
Live in the light.

Grief is a painful
part of the journey through life.
Some of us are just less fortunate
and have to endure unnatural losses
like a child.
Others suffer greatly also when they lose
parents or siblings or spouses.
No one gets a pass when it comes to grief.
It's a part of life
and love.
and It's a part of
the journey.

Birds are fragile,
just like life,
and they are beautiful,
just like life.
Life is fragile
but we are not.
We are strong and resilient
and can live with our pain and still see
the beauty of life because we are strong!
Please don't let your grief break you
because you still have a beautiful life ahead
if you choose
that path.

I had a terrible argument
with someone
I love very much.
It took me two days to regain my balance.
I am strong, but I am fragile
and I'm not ashamed to admit that.
We have been burned
deeply by our loss.
The depth of all of our feelings are felt more strongly now.
That's just a fact
of grief.

Especially in grief
it's important to
surround yourself with lightness.
Do what feeds your hurt soul
as much as you can.
For me, it's working with color.
For you it might be music.
Whatever brings your mind
and heart peace
or joy
will bring you closer to your departed
love because your loved one
is not in the darkness but in the
light.

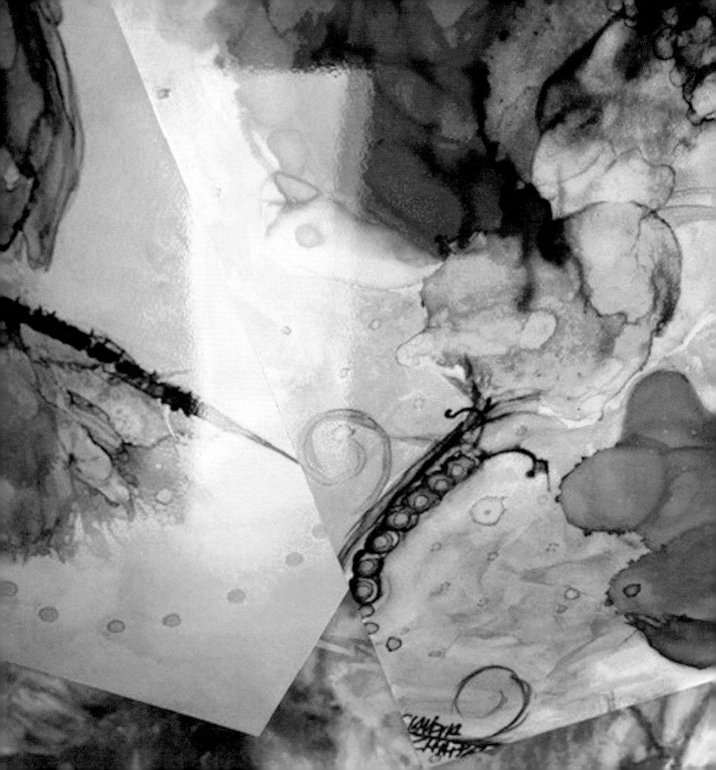

Survival
through creativity
was my first discovery
and it still holds true today.
Find what gives you peace
and nurtures your soul.
Healing will come
in time.

Thank God for pets.
They fill the heart
and soul
with peace
and love.
This one sensed my sadness
and never left my side.
I am grateful for him
and gratitude is
healing.

Some days
on this journey we actually
notice the flowers.
Those are welcomed days.
Don't feel guilty
when you feel good.
You need to let yourself
feel good sometimes
in order to survive.

All living things grow
towards the light.

Heaven
in the summertime.
That's what this painting
makes me think.
I had a dream one night
a few weeks after Ben died.
To this day I believe he was taking me
to see where he was.
The colors were incredibly vibrant
and my feelings were euphoric.
He always wanted me
to see what he was looking at and
feel what he was feeling.
This still gives me a sense of comfort
that I know he's
okay.

A year ago
I went to the wedding of my dear friend's son.
I was so happy for her.
Feelings of anger started drifting up on the first day
of this glorious weekend.
I have learned over these years how to console
and reason with myself.
I had to first acknowledge
that the anger I was feeling was my grief.
Deep grief never goes away. We learn to live with it.
It becomes a part of the fabric of our lives.
We can learn to live and even enjoy our life when we
find our strength.

Everyday on this journey
is a secret
until we begin our day.
Some days are filled with color
other days are misty and gloomy,
even that's needed sometimes
for rest.
Sometimes we need to stop
trying to live
and just be.

I paint a lot of pathways,
journeys.
I paint life even though death is a huge part of what
motivates me to live.
I have to Choose life everyday.
When you lose your loved one to death,
A huge part of yourself dies also.
At some point you realize you have to choose life
for yourself
and those who love and need you.
Also,
you never know who else is also
choosing life.

In the Fall
we watch the leaves turn colors
and the air get cold.
For us it's
a reminder of another year
without
our departed loved one.
In nature, death is beautiful,
not in life,
but know that love doesn't die.
We still love them and they still love us.

We read about the stages of grief
as if it were neat,
orderly
and predictable.
In reality it is a messy myriad
of pain,
shock and sometimes peace if that person was suffering.
Eventually, you will grow to accept
the reality of your loss
and learn to find joy again
in spite of it
as you grow
stronger.

It always thrills me
to see the resilience
of life.
Just like grass through the snow
or a flower through a city pavement,
We too will break through
the cold
and frozen hardship of grief
because life strives
to live.

Birthdays, Anniversaries,
Mother's and Father's Day.
These days are just sad
when you're not able
to wrap your arms around
that person.
All you can do is honor them
in the way
that helps you
get through the day.
These days pass in
24 hours.

My grief is a part of me now.
It is okay to leave it home when I go away for a few days.
It's so necessary to take a break
from all of it occasionally.
It does not mean
that you have stopped grieving,
or loving,
only that you need some time to rejuvenate and find
a little peace for your grieving heart and soul.
What we seek is
strength.

I for one am always relieved
when the "Holidays"
are over.
During the holiday season
I find it challenging
to keep myself strong.
We watch all the merriment around us,
it's hard to avoid.
Deep grief is a winding and
bumpy road.
At some point we need to pick ourselves back up and
continue forward.

The sun will set
and then rise again tomorrow.
We made it through
another Holiday
without our beloved.
I don't think they ever get easier,
we just learn that they pass
and we pick up our lives again tomorrow.
I know my son loves me
and wants me to live and laugh and love
until I join him.

Spring is here.
Life goes on with or without us.
Choose life for now.
Our departed loved one
will be waiting for us on the other side
when our time on earth is up.
We still have many seasons to be alive.
Choose life.

It is possible
to feel the warmth of sunshine
and see the beauty in life
while we are grieving.
Deep losses are grieved for the rest of your life.
We can learn
how to live fully
even with our pain.
It just becomes another part of the fabric of ourselves
and our journey.

Gratitude
isn't an emotion most grief stricken people
feel.
But you can.
Only then can you start the healing process.
I'm referring to gratitude for the other loves
we have in our lives here.
What most people don't understand
about the process
is that it is a challenging
lifelong journey.

As the warmer weather approaches
it's important to nurture your heart
by being outside.
Surround yourselves with life.
For those of us
who feel like we have one foot on earth
and the other in heaven,
I think it's critical.

Grief is a journey
that has no end.
The destination is
Survival.

Life is a gift.
Sometimes it takes a loss
to remind us of that.
Both pain and joy
are a part of life.
It isn't possible to have one without the other.
We only feel pain to the depth that we are able to feel joy.
Both are a natural part of life.
Acceptance.

Benjamin Chappel
1979-2006

Notes

ABOUT THE AUTHOR / ARTIST

A successful professional artist, Claudia, a single mom, supported her children by painting tiles for peoples' homes. It allowed her to be home with her children. Then, at the age of 53, Claudia experienced the unimaginable. She answered a knock at the door and a policeman was standing there. He told her every parent's worst nightmare: her son Ben, the first love of her life, was gone.

After Ben's death, she fell into a dark and lonely place. She gave up painting. Over the next 13 years, Claudia slowly learned to live with her pain and grief. She began to paint again. Her work had no special meaning to her at the time.

Anyone who has experienced the death of a loved one began to seek her out for advice, comfort and hope. Over time Claudia realized that she was saying the same words repeatedly, so she decided to write them down. It wasn't until she began writing her first book that she realized the art, which she thought had no meaning, served as perfect illustrations.

Her first book was initially written as a gift for a mother whose son had recently died. Other's wanted copies to send to friends who were suffering the same losses, so she started making copies. The growing response indicated a need to publish the book more traditionally, and soon people who were grieving the deaths of spouses and parents and other loved ones were sharing that first book. This demand inspired this new book, which is meant to help a broader audience process their grief. Helping others gives purpose to both Claudia's grief and her art.

Claudia lives in Baltimore, Maryland with her loving husband Richard and close to her daughter Jessica, son-in-law Michael and two grandchildren, Olive and Gus. Her loves also include her two dogs and two birds.